SCRIBBLES OF THE UNASHAMED

BY

TOSIN DA-SILVA

DEDICATION

Dedicated to the broken woman who is
finding strength to carry on

The Vulnerable place

Can you love my ugly?
Are you still down for me if I show you my
weakness?
Would you still look at me the same way if
you saw the things I struggled with?
Would your love for me wax stronger
knowing my brokenness?
You see I cover my weakness because I
fear once you see the real me you will flee.
But I long to show the real me. I long to
show the me without the mask.
A lot of times people love our good sides
but are not ready to love our other sides.
They ain't ready to love you through your
processes.
'Love covers a multiple of sin', they say; but
today's love doesn't know how to love one
through scars and brokenness.
You see, I carry a lot of cuts and bruises,
and my 'make up' covers them so well.
I hide it with my bitch face, snide remarks
and arrogant attitude.
I'd rather you look at me and see a tough
woman, than pity my vulnerability.

But deep down, I yearn for someone to look and see me, see my ugly yet still love me... clean my cuts and bruises where they're festering, and help them heal. Deep down, I want to be whole but I don't know how to be...
So I'll ask again can you love my ugly

BRUISED

"Hush! If you tell anyone what happened I will kill you. Besides no one will believe you," he said as he pulled her dress down with a wicked grin on his face
Too scared to say a word, she sobbed in silence. She was shocked, petrified at what her 'Uncle' did. She was just 7, and she couldn't understand why he touched her there. Too timid was she to say a word so she 'hushed' and said nothing...
but the older she got the more she felt unclean.
"I mean, there must be something wrong with me for this to happen over and over," she thought.
She grew up into a young woman who felt her body was a play thing for men.
Bruised and broken she was... but no one could see what was inside.
All they saw was the body count going up...
"Ashawo!"
That's what they said behind her and to her face, and she bought it.

Constantly seeking for attention from men because she felt only a man could validate her.
Stripped of her self esteem and self worth, and barely existing; because inside was numb and cold.
"Is there anyone who will love me for me, not my body, but for me," she cried out when she hit rock bottom...
"I do," whispered the Still Voice. "I always have."
But she wasn't having it.
How could HE love her when she was so unworthy?
She tried to run,
But Yahweh had no intention of letting her go.
"Give me your pain, give me your fears, give it all to me," He said, looking into her eyes with so much ccompassion And one by one, she did -
Laying it all at His feet till she began to heal from the bruises and see herself as He did...
a Queen, righteous, worthy, beautiful and totally wanted by Abba.

SHAME

Shame.
That was all she felt as the man she thought
was a friend lay on top of her.
Shame and helplessness she had never felt
before rode over her.
Why did I come here? Why didn't I just stay
at home? she thought.
She struggled to push him away, but he
was stronger so she gave in, and he took
what she had placed so much pride in.
She could neither cry nor scream as shame
washed over her.
I caused this, was all she thought.
From that day, shame wrapped around her
like a warm blanket that she never took off.
She wore it everywhere.
It affected whatever decision she took, and
for a long time, it was all she knew till she
met HIM....
He who looked at her and saw her!
Really saw her!
He didn't see the whore who could not
protect her dignity.
He didn't see the girl who let her desire rule
her.

He saw her!
The girl who needed to be loved.
And He wooed her.
He chased her wholeheartedly, and like a flower opening up to the sunshine, she opened up to His love, till she saw what He saw beneath:
A Diamond!
Rough on the surface, but after processing, one that would shine brightly.
She traded her shame for His love.

The Warrior Princess

"You are pregnant."
No! she screamed in her head
This can't be happening right now!
Looking down at her still flat stomach,
petrified with fear
How can I bring this little one into the world
and protect it? I can't. She thought.
Scared and alone, she made up her mind
not to keep it.
But Abba wasn't having that.
"I am here.
This is not for you to carry alone;
I am with you.
"You are both mine!" He thundered
jealously.
She fought hard.
She wanted to run away
"I am not ready, I can't handle this...
I am not worthy"
But no matter how she fought, He held them
both, till she gave in.

Each day her belly grew; the life within her was so precious.
The bigger the belly, the more she was in awe.
The day she pushed forth her child, she heard her before she saw her: loud, deep and strong like the warrior princess she was.
Then she held her, eyes so captivating it took her breathe away, eyes that looked up to her.
Ten fingers, ten toes, she counted.
She watched her little warrior try to latch on as she nursed, and she knew without a doubt that she would love this one all her days.
She would fight for her, protect her and give her all she could.
This beautiful gift that came out of her mess.

DEAR GOD

"Dear God, it happened again. I know I said I wouldn't, but I did. I thought I could handle it. I know you are disgusted with me; I'm disgusted with myself! What kind of child claims to love her Father and blatantly disrespects him? I'm such a horrid child, wanton and I have no respect! I've no idea why you love me, I can't love myself! I've failed you over and over again, like I've not learnt my lessons. This flesh of mine, what do I do with it?! Father forgive me..."
Those were the words she poured out in her dairy, in anguish, disgusted at how weak she was.
The still voice of the Holy Spirit whispered, "You are forgiven, receive the Father's love."
But so caught up was she in her guilt, that she allowed the enemy to deceive her.
She was unclean, unworthy and definitely unrighteous.
She forgot that when Christ died on the cross it was because of her, and she was the righteousness of God in Christ Jesus.

But you see, Abba loved her so much, He didn't give up trying to reach this broken daughter of His.
He sent a word!
Oh, how she broke down and wept when she heard it! She had been carrying the burden of self-loath for so long, she'd forgotten the Father's love is like a river - ever flowing.
She ran with arms wide open to the One who loved her completely.
The warmth of His embrace melted her walls, and He began the healing in her, through her and with her.

THE SIDE CHIC

She was pampered silly by this man who abandoned his wife at home.
He made her feel like she was the only girl in the world, so she dulled the still little voice and became the other woman she swore she would never be.
Private meetings, exotic dinners and lavish shopping was how he maintained her, and she enjoyed every bit of it, oblivious to the other woman's pain.
Since she couldn't get a man, she decided to settle for the taken man who came knocking.
Everyday he would leave her to go be with his wife and anger would fill her heart; she sent him home with tantrums and a sulky attitude every night.
She began to want more. She didn't want to be just the other woman in his life anymore, she wanted to be the only woman - and that became her obsession.
When she realised all his sweet words were poison to her soul and he was never going to leave his wife for her, she broke down.

She was just his side chic, nothing more, nothing less.
Anguish in her heart, she realised she had shot herself in the foot loving a man who wasn't hers in the first place.
That still voice she constantly silenced spoke louder than ever,
"Walk away my child, come home to me."
She walked away from the married man: she had been a captive of the little he offered her for too long.
Like a blind woman receiving her sight, she saw the hurt she had caused the other woman, and guilt set in.
...but the still voice of Abba reminded her He still loved her. If He could forgive her, she could forgive herself.
That day a burden lifted off her shoulders and the healing began.

BUTTERFLIES

Butterflies, that's what he gave her.
Butterflies fluttering in her belly just at the sound of his voice.
Even more intense butterflies, everytime she saw him.
You see, he was like a tall glass of chocolate - so fine you literally forgot to breathe.
He entered the room and commanded everyone's attention. Girls wanted to be with him and guys wanted to be him.
It was a shocker when he chose her 'Plain Jane'.
She was so lovestruck that she said yes without hesitating.
He had all her 'mumu' buttons, and he pressed them at will.
He was her sun, moon and stars;
Alas, she was just his plaything, nurse and maid.
She was too blinded by love to see that was all he saw.
Her love was deaf and blind and dumb to his flaws.

She became an empty shell of herself just to please him... after all, he was her sun, moon and stars.
A voice deep within kept telling her to 'leave, leave, leave!' But she shut it down every time.
How could she leave the one she loved?
Not until his love had her dried up and broken, did her eyes open to see that the face he showed was only a gold-plated surface that gave way to rusted iron deep within.
It dawned on her much too late that the butterflies she felt were nothing but hunger pangs for something that wasn't meant to be.
A hunger called lust which had her broken and torn.
The day she walked away, was the day she got her freedom...
No looking back!!!

THE UNREQUITED LOVE

The worst thing a woman can put herself
through is unrequited love.
She gives him her all: spirit, soul and body,
and hungers for him to love her as much as
she loves him
He tells her 'give me time', so she remains
loyal to a man who isn't hers.
She loves him completely and he gives her
a portion of his love; just enough to keep
her staying on.
Month after month, she prays that this is the
one he loves her completely, but month
after month the less his love is.
Her mind tells her to flee, for she was
worthy of so much more...
But her heart, oh her heart, can't see past
him.
She sees the potential of the love he could
give her if only he would open up to her,
She stays longing for him to love her so.
Then one day, as she looks in the mirror,
the Still Quiet Voice says to her,
"How long? How long will you cast your
pearls before swine? Have you forgotten
who you are? You are a Queen! A king

recognises his queen when he sees her!
She doesn't beg for his attention, she
commands it!"
That's the fateful day she straightened
crown and her shoulders and let him go.
It wasn't the easiest decision she made and
it was a journey to heal,
But that day she crossed the line, and there
was no backing out

THE ONE WHO SMILES

She is pretty and calm
Beautiful to behold
A good friend
She listens and gives great advice
She is the friend you run to when you are in crisis, because she always has a word of encouragement or a word of advice to help in that crisis
The world sees her as a strong the strong one
A smile on her face always
But you see behind that smile is a broken spirit
What the world sees is just a facade
She has had many years of practice to mask her hurt and pain
The world sees a happy woman but in her closet is a broken woman
No one sees her pain because she won't let them close enough to see
She doesn't see what the world sees
She looks in the mirror and sees a shattered woman
Night after night she cries herself to sleep contemplating if life is worth living

Morning after morning she rises with a smile
and faces the world as a dutiful daughter
and friend
For a long time she carried her burden on
her own, not letting anyone see her struggle
Until she encountered Him
On that day she broke down and cried like a
little girl, and the world was in shock to see
her so!
Every burden she lay before Him, every
brokenness she let Him see, every flaw she
opened for Him to see
And what a beautiful sight to see her
vulnerable
For in her vulnerability she glowed
She let the world see who she really was,
and drew many as she did

INSECURE

"You have added weight!"
"Girl, when will you hit the gym?"
"This tummy though, what are we doing
about it?"
"Don't wear that, all your tyres are on
display."
"Try this herbal tea, it will help you shed
weight."
Round face
Round body
Skin too dark
Comments left, right and centre
Unsolicited advice given everywhere she
turned
They made her feel she wasn't good
enough
So she thrived to be good enough
Diet here, weight loss there
Corset here, girdle there
She avoided mirrors, they reminded her of
how ugly her body was
Smirks and snide remarks here and there
The way people looked at her was enough
to remind her; she didn't need a mirror to
add to it

Her self-confidence whittled away
She got to the point she loathed her body
The One who created her asked her,
"What are you doing?"
"I am trying to change me," she answered
"Why?"
"Because I'm ugly."
"But my darling, you are beautiful whatever
body size you are.
This body I created has carried a child,
nursed it and been through various things.
Your body is a reminder that you are not
just a survivor, but a warrior.
Every inch of you is beautiful!
Besides changing your body isn't the source
of your joy, I am!
If you can't find joy in me, absolutely
nothing you do to that gorgeous body of
yours will make you happy.
So embrace your body my child ,as I have."
She rose up and looked in the mirror for the
first time in ages, and saw what He saw.

THAT GIRL

Waist beads on her hips
A chain on her ankle
Stud on her nose
Two more piercing on her earlobes
Coloured lens in her eyes
6 inches heels on her feet
Waist length Brazilian hair on her head
She turned heads as she entered any room
because she looked good and knew how to
walk gracefully in heels.
Whispers and snickers from other women
as she passed by,
"This one must be a heathen; how can a
Christian wear anklet fa? Have you seen
what's on her nose! No child of God can
have such! God forbid!"
Those were the responses from women
who felt they were more righteous than she
was
Unknown to them, baby girl was a warrior in
heels
She took her time to look good but spent
more time in the battle room
She was the righteousness of God through
Christ Jesus

She who could slay dragons as she could slay in fashion
What they didn't know was her ministry and those she ministered to
You see, she drew women who slayed in fashion but were empty, and she pulled them to Christ
She opened their eyes to see that a fashionista is absolutely nothing without Christ
Her light shone so brightly that they wanted to know her God - and that was what she was called to do
To raise Queens out of the pit, who could take their places in the Kingdom and slay in between

HIM

She was busy with her Father's work, loving
life and just living for Him
She had come to a place where she was
whole and complete without a man
She had given up on ever having one so
she dedicated herself to her calling, thinking
that was all she was made for
Then he showed up
She didn't notice him at first for who he was
meant to be to her
He was just her buddy like every other guy
friend she had - or so she thought!
You see he had no intention of staying a
buddy
He knew she was his and he was hers, and
even though she was clueless to that, he
was determined she saw who he was
So he crept into her heart bit by bit
Pulling down the walls she had built
overtime from constant heartbreak
He was determined to show her he was
going nowhere and was willing to wait for
her
Never had she met someone so relentless
and so sure she was his

She ran to the Father and argued why it
couldn't be
Listed all her flaws, all her shortcomings, all
her screw ups in the past, and how she was
good all by herself
The Father smiled and said,
"My beloved, but you will be better with him.
One puts to flight a thousand; two, tens of
thousands.
I didn't create you to be alone beloved, you
were created to fulfill purpose with him.
Alone you have achieved so much, but
together you will achieve more than you
could hope or imagine.
If you reject him, you reject Me."
So she opened her heart to him
And my goodness! What a sight to see her
glow in his love
God's reflection of just how much He loved
her
And together, they conquered the world!

RECKLESS LOVER

Eyes like fire
Laughter like thunder
Voice like the sounding of a thousand
rainfalls
Face which shines as brightly as the sun
That's my lover
Have you met Him?
Let me tell you about Him
My lover has had eyes for me from the
beginning of time
He has loved me before I was born
The day I was born His eyes lit up with joy,
"Finally, she is here."
My lover patiently waited for me to grow up
so I could be His
My lover is a patient gentleman
I, on the other hand, am not so patient:
I sought other lovers,
Trying to fill the void only meant for my lover
But no matter how many lovers I had, no
one could fill that void
My lover still waited
He followed me everywhere longing for me
to see him

When I was in danger, my lover would show
up and wage war for my sake
But still I ignored my lover even as He
fought silently for me
Each day He would reach out to me and
each day I would turn Him down
Then one day I looked into the eyes of my
lover, about to turn Him down one more
time
And I saw myself in His eyes
Shivers ran through my body, and I knew
that He was what I had been looking for all
this time!
His eyes told me He loved me!
Unconditionally, passionately, recklessly
and completely
Oh, His eyes told me I was home!
I was done being a runaway bride
So that day I walked into my lover's arms
The arms in which I was to be forever.

Selah.

ABOUT THE AUTHOR

Oluwatosin da-silva is a daughter of Abba and Fashion designer who writes on the side. She is also mum to a little princess and   has found purpose in helping young women heal from their emotional hurts having been through similar situations.